WOMEN WITH SECRETS

WOMEN WITH SECRETS

Dealing with Domestic Abuse And Childhood Sexual Abuse in Treatment

Cathy Skrip
Kristin Kunzman

 HAZELDEN®

First published August 1991.

ISBN: 0-89486-771-7
Library of Congress Catalog Card Number: 91-72475

Printed in the United States of America.

Editor's note:
   Hazelden Educational Materials offers a variety of information on chemical dependency and related areas. Our publications do not necessarily represent Hazelden's programs, nor do they officially speak for any Twelve Step organization.

About the book:

   As a chemical dependency counselor, have you sometimes felt you were missing pieces of the puzzle when treating certain women clients? A background of domestic abuse or childhood sexual abuse may have been those puzzle pieces. This book provides tools for reading the signs of abuse—both childhood sexual and domestic—and for making good aftercare referrals to help these women build a healthy sobriety.

About the authors:

   Kristin Kunzman is the author of a book, *The Healing Way: Adult Recovery from Childhood Sexual Abuse,* and a pamphlet, *Healing from Childhood Sexual Abuse,* both Hazelden Educational Materials publications. She is a psychologist practicing in Minneapolis.
   Cathy Skrip is a psychologist and is co-founder of the Abuse Resource Center, a family violence educational consulting firm, in St. Paul.

Contents

PART I
Dealing With Domestic Abuse in Treatment 5

Cathy Skrip

Women who are battered and are in treatment carry a double load of shame and fear. The enormity of those feelings can interfere with their treatment and get in the way of healthy sobriety. But it doesn't have to be that way. The counselor, once equipped with knowledge of the problem, can play a role by offering these women education about the cycle of abuse and then by directing them to helpful aftercare referrals. Part I offers the tools to help accomplish this.

PART II

Dealing with Childhood
Sexual Abuse in Treatment 41

Kristin Kunzman

Another secret often carried by women in recovery is a history of childhood sexual abuse. Approximately one of every three women reports having been sexually abused before the age of eighteen. Many women entering treatment may only suspect they have been abused. Once the chemicals are gone, they may begin having memories of the abuse. That remembering process will not necessarily happen in treatment, but treatment counselors can help even women who only suspect they have been abused—by offering them education about the healing process, and by helping them connect with psychotherapists who specialize in working with survivors of childhood sexual abuse. Part II effectively illustrates how chemical dependency counselors can help set these survivors on the path to recovery from childhood sexual abuse, as well as guide them to healthy sobriety.

Acknowledgments

Special thanks to Mary Ann Palumbo and Signe Masterson, my associates at the Abuse Resource Center, for their support and involvement in writing this booklet.

— CATHY SKRIP

I would like to thank all my co-workers over the years at Relate Counseling Center, Synergy, Metropolitan Clinic of Counseling, and Franklin Psychiatric Clinic. They shared generously their knowledge and encouragement in the fields of chemical dependency and childhood sexual abuse. They have taught me much and I am very grateful.

— KRISTIN KUNZMAN

Introduction

This book is directed to those whose primary area of expertise is working with victims of alcohol and other substance abuse. If you are a chemical dependency professional, you undoubtedly know that most substance abuse problems don't exist independently of other major social issues and concerns. You look at the whole person even as you focus on her chemical dependency. Domestic abuse and childhood sexual abuse have been combined in one publication for three reasons: (1) many women in treatment are victims of domestic violence and/or childhood sexual abuse; (2) the family's symptoms and the ramifications of those symptoms in the lives of the victims are quite similar; and (3) abuse tends to be carried as a big secret by its victims, a secret that feeds alienation, builds walls, creates shame, and sometimes leads to relapse to chemical use.

Any of your clients may have experienced or witnessed sexual abuse or domestic violence as a child. Conversely, we in the area of sexual abuse and domestic abuse treatment see a large percentage of clients who abuse alcohol and other drugs. They may use and abuse situationally as a way to cope with feelings, low self-esteem, and hopelessness, or they may be true addicts and alcoholics. One way or another, their use cannot be overlooked. Until these women eliminate the alcohol and other drug abuse from their lives, they are usually not ready to work on the abuse or violence issues. Most women who are struggling with both chemical dependency and abuse issues are likely to feel quite hopeless and generally feel like "bad" people. When their struggles with the problems resulting from childhood sexual abuse and domestic violence are recognized and acknowledged, they are more likely to benefit from chemical dependency treatment as positively as those clients who are struggling primarily with substance abuse problems.

The information in this book can help you to identify members of this population more easily. As you learn of their problems, you can be more effective in helping them build trust and a good base for maintaining sobriety. This book will also provide you with information and tools for reading the signs of abuse and making good referrals after treatment.

Your ability to understand and validate their negative experiences and to make knowledgeable referrals for help with issues of sexual abuse and domestic violence can make treatment a more positive and hopeful experience for these women, as well as make their continuing care and sobriety much more effective.

— THE AUTHORS

PART I

Dealing with Domestic Abuse in Treatment

Cathy Skrip

Domestic abuse is a crime. It is underreported, minimized, and denied, both by those directly involved and by society in general. It is as invisible as it is invasive. It does not respect any boundaries, categories, or limitations. Occurring behind the closed door of "home sweet home," it is often a closely guarded family secret. The perpetrators and survivors of this insidious crime look like Everyman and Everywoman.

Have you, as a chemical health professional, ever worked with a recovering woman over an extended period and been frustrated by watching her relapse again and again? Have you ever wondered why some people are in greater crisis after reaching sobriety than they were while using? Have you questioned why the support systems and traditional interventions that work so well for some recovering individuals don't work for others? Have you sometimes sensed that you were missing a piece of the puzzle, but couldn't find it no matter how hard you searched?

In many cases, the missing piece is the presence of domestic abuse or some other form of family violence. This portion of our book is intended to help you meet the following objectives:

- Add a clearer understanding of the unique dynamics of domestic abuse to your existing knowledge of substance abuse.
- Explore the relationship between domestic abuse and substance abuse.
- Offer specific tools for integrating the healing process for survivors of domestic as well as substance abuse.

You might feel that your expertise in the field of chemical health is enough and that you cannot be expected to take on responsibility for every other social issue that needs to be addressed by your multi-symptom clients. In reality, taking the time to understand the dynamics of domestic abuse will make your job easier. While you don't need to assume total responsibility for treating domestic abuse, your intervention for chemical dependency will be more effective if you're able to recognize and acknowledge the presence of domestic abuse in a client's life.

Statistics generally acknowledge that at least six million American women a year are beaten by their partners. The Federal Bureau of Investigation's reports have estimated that one American woman in two will experience domestic violence at some time during her life. Thirty-four percent of female homicide victims older than fifteen are killed by their husbands or intimate partners. One woman in four is pregnant when beaten, and the average battered wife is attacked three times each year.[1,2,3,4]

Substance abuse may mask domestic abuse. Conversely, domestic violence may draw attention away from chemical abuse problems, or it may be used to rationalize chemical use as a necessary medication for the pain. It is estimated that 45 percent of women in treatment for alcoholism were battered women who eventually became alcohol-dependent.[5] Estimates of the percentage of batterers who assault their partners while intoxicated range from 48 percent to 87 percent, with most of the research indicating a 60 to 70 percent rate of alcohol abuse and a 13 to 20 percent rate of other drug abuse among these batterers.[6]

The information in this book is meant to help you see telltale signs of domestic abuse that would otherwise go unnoticed in a client. Some of the examples used will refer to survivors of abuse as women and to abusers as men. This tendency reflects a variety of studies indicating that 97 percent of abuse victims are female and also draws on the author's experience of working primarily with women.[7] Furthermore, when assaults occur between partners, it is the woman who is injured by a man in 95 percent of the cases.[8] It is important to remember, however, that men are abused by women and that domestic abuse does happen in gay and lesbian relationships.

The dynamics that govern domestic abuse also apply to other forms of family violence and some types of sexual assault. While this section of the book will focus on domestic abuse as a distinct type of family violence, that distinction may become artificial as you work with clients. It is highly likely that a woman involved in an abusive domestic relationship may also have experienced child abuse, childhood sexual abuse, neglect, or sexual harassment.

What Is Domestic Abuse?

For the purposes of working with clients, *domestic abuse* may be defined as any exploitive or threatening behaviors intended to harm or exert power or control over another family or household member. Abuse may be emotional, physical, sexual, or economic, including, but not limited, to the following:

Emotional Abuse

Mind games, name-calling, constant criticizing, withholding approval or affection as punishment, public or private humiliation, abusing pets, threatening, manipulating, blaming.

Physical Abuse

Pushing, slapping, kicking, choking, locking out of house, threatening with weapon, harassing to the point of physical illness, restraining, depriving of sleep, biting, shaking, spitting.

Sexual Abuse

Raping, withholding sex and affection, unwanted or inappropriate touch, sex after beating or illness, sexual criticism, forcing sex in front of others, treating others as sex objects, sadistic sexual acts.

Economic Abuse

Refusing to work or share money, hiding checkbook or credit cards, refusing to pay bills, taking back gifts, exploiting assets, using money to manipulate, hiding money made through self-employment.

For legal purposes, domestic abuse is defined more narrowly and differs from state to state. Legal definitions naturally focus on the more tangible physical and sexual forms of abuse. In your work, it is important to encourage clients not to minimize the more subtle forms of abuse and not to underestimate the long-term consequences of any type of abuse. Women who have moved from physically violent relationships to "only" emotionally violent relationships may need reminders that they do not deserve *any* abuse. With a few exceptions, most experts agree that abuse is a learned behavior, but violence during childhood does not predetermine adult violence. Experts who have reviewed the research estimate about a 30 percent rate of intergenerational transmission of violence.[9] Recent thinking indicates that witnessing family violence or being neglected during childhood may predict these adult behaviors just as strongly as actually being abused.[10]

Three Phases of Domestic Abuse

An abuser's greatest need is to manipulate and control others. While the abuse may be constant or sporadic, the abuser will generally establish a pattern of a tension-building phase, a violent-incident phase, and then a calming phase. The word *pattern* is important in distinguishing a person with abusive behaviors from an *abuser*. For example, we have probably all called another person a derogatory name at some time. While this is an abusive behavior, it does not, in and of itself, make us abusers.

The Tension Builds

As an abusive pattern begins, tension is typically generated by ordinary day-to-day events such as menu choices, cleanliness of the house, disciplining of the children, job pressures, or unresolved arguments. If you entered an abuser's home as an outside, uninformed observer during this phase, you would probably not notice anything amiss. This phase could last for a few seconds, or it could last for an extended period of time, or it might not exist at all—everyone's pattern is different.

The Abuser Lashes Out

Eventually, the tension mounts to the point of violent incidents. During this second phase, the abuser "lets off steam" by deliberately lashing out to create fear and chaos and to take absolute control over the situation. Contrary to popular belief, the abuser is not out of control at this point but, rather, is in total control.

Then the Calm

After the violent incident, a calming phase might begin and the abuser may apologize, increase affection, buy gifts, or find other ways to convince the person being abused that "it will never happen again." As the progression continues, the tension-building and calming phases may become shorter or may disappear altogether, and the violence may become more severe.

Riding a Roller Coaster

To help clients understand the progressions of violence committed by abusers, you might ask them to keep journals, document incidents chronologically, or use visualizations. The analogy of riding a roller coaster may be helpful to some, although it is important for chemical dependency clients not to equate the thrill of roller coaster riding with the high of using chemicals. Ask your clients to describe their physical, emotional, and intellectual responses from the time they begin to approach the roller coaster. As they board the ride and inch their way to the top, they may report physical sensations such as general body tension, sweaty palms, clenched jaws, or a nervous stomach. Emotionally, they may feel scared, anxious, or numb. Intellectual self-talk might include any of the following: "*Why* am I doing this?" "Whatever happens, I don't want to look like a chicken!" "I said I would go on this ride so there's no turning back now!" "Millions of people ride roller coasters each year, and they survive."

The climb to the first peak is analogous to the tension-building phase of abuse. Ask your client to recall her abuser's latest violent outburst and then to think back to the initial feelings of rising tension prior to that incident. If this is difficult to pinpoint, focus your client's attention back to getting on the roller coaster. We all have unique ways of experiencing tension, but it is likely that our reactions to diverse stresses have some similarities. For example, a woman who states that she would have a headache as she boarded the roller coaster might also have a headache fifteen minutes before her partner's expected arrival home from work. Helping clients tune in to these subtle physical, emotional, and intellectual cues can empower them with a greater sense of self-control and can also protect them by giving some time for logical thinking prior to the point of crisis.

The violent-incident phase is like reaching the top of the roller coaster's peak and knowing there is no choice but to take the plunge. The rider has absolutely no control at this point, other than hanging on and surviving. Compared to the painfully slow ride up to the peak, the plunge may actually come as a relief, since the rider knows the worst will, at least temporarily, be over. Likewise, in some abusive relationships, the tension-building phase is actually more stressful to the survivor than the violence, and so this person may purposely aggravate the abuser in order to get it over with. This common, but rather contradictory, dynamic may confuse even the survivor into thinking that she "asked for it."

Over time, the person being abused, like the seasoned roller coaster rider, will develop very effective survival skills. Physically, the survivor may be hypervigilant, numb, or very tense during the violent-incident phase. The person's emotions may range from helplessness and fear to aggressiveness. Intellectual self-talk might include any of the following: "I wonder if I will live through this?" "I've had enough. I'm never going to let this happen again." "If I had just done things differently, this wouldn't have happened."

Once the roller coaster begins its plummet, the rider gradually relaxes and rides it out. She may loosen her grip, relax her muscles, and release her tension by screaming. Emotionally, she may feel an overwhelming sense of relief. There may be feelings of thankfulness or even pride for having survived the ride, or there might be feelings of determination never to go on another roller coaster. Intellectually, the person might be thinking any of the following: "I made it through that one!" "I guess it could have been worse!" "I suppose I shouldn't complain since I did agree to go on the ride."

In your work, you may want to encourage clients to come up with their own visualizations or chart their own roller coaster rides, and you will want to assure them that their personal experiences of violence may not fit any of the classic models.

Who Does Domestic Abuse Involve?

Domestic abuse involves us all. If we are not abusing or being abused in our personal relationships, we may still be affected by the abusive experiences of our friends or relatives. As taxpayers or employers, we are affected because violence at home leads to high absenteeism, high turnover, and low productivity in the workplace. The dynamics of abuse give fuel to sexism, racism, and classism; the practice of domestic abuse instructs our children to grow up repeating the same patterns. As a society, our responsibility is to stop condoning abuse; and as a professional person, you can begin by telling your clients that abuse is never OK.

Many stereotypes exist about the people directly involved in domestic abuse. In the author's experience of talking to groups, batterers are most often seen as male, Caucasian, tall, dark, mustachioed, underemployed or jobless, and poorly educated. Batterers are also seen as people who wear jeans and flannel shirts, drive motorcycles, and use vulgar language. Occasionally, audiences will identify just the opposite: small, well-groomed men in three-piece suits who drive Mercedes and head their own businesses. Similarly, people being abused are stereotyped as female, small, thin, pale, light-haired, plainly dressed but clean, high-school educated, employed, and submissive.

These perceptions are both right and wrong, since any person you see on the street could be involved in an abusive relationship at home. In fact, survivors whose abusers have high economic or social status and defy the stereotypes may have extreme difficulty being believed when they finally gather the courage to share their stories. Helping professionals need to realize that their own stereotypical views of abuse may be no different from those of the general population. Since society more readily condones male abuse of females, male members of the chemical dependency team will need to develop special sensitivity when working with female clients, and organizations will want to support separate programming for men and women.

As you work with female clients who have been abusive, you will typically find them overwhelmed by feelings of blame and shame. These feelings may be compounded by the blame and shame already attached to their use of chemicals. Male clients with similar experience will typically focus attention on their mate's violence while minimizing their own. In some abusive relationships, both partners may become violent, and you may need to help clients understand the concept of the *primary aggressor.* This legal term is not used in all states, but the concept helps differentiate between using abusive behavior and being an abuser and connotes a difference in motivation or intent. The degree or fear of injury and the history of abuse are both used to determine the primary physical aggressor, and the intent of this determination is to protect the survivor.

For example, an abuser may constantly give his partner the message that he will kill her if she does not meet his expectations. He may reinforce this verbal message in a variety of nonverbal ways, such as constantly cleaning his guns, talking about his skill in marksmanship, building a wooden casket in the basement that is just her size, or lifting weights to increase his strength. As this woman begins to accept the fact that her mate really could kill her, she may begin to think more about her own defense. If her fear level becomes high enough during the next physical or sexual assault, she may strike back physically. The husband in this scenario is still the primary aggressor.

How Are Domestic Abuse And Substance Abuse Related?

The famous question of "What came first, the chicken or the egg?" suggests the complexity of the relationship between domestic abuse and substance abuse. No firm conclusions about this relationship can yet be drawn, since much of the research done has been contradictory or inconclusive. While substance abuse is often given as an explanation for violence, domestic abuse is just as frequently cited as the cause of battered women's chemical addiction. While the two problems may appear to be inextricably intertwined, it is essential that you, as a chemical health professional, recognize them as two distinct problems. Since violent behavior is not caused by substance abuse, it follows that violence will not cease just because sobriety is attained.

Numerous studies reporting high alcohol use by abusers found that the battered women in these situations fell within the normal range for alcohol use among women.[11] Researchers Kaufman, Kantor, and Straus found that women who drink heavily have a higher likelihood of minor domestic assaults than other women, but substance abuse of any type by women is not a significant factor in severe violence. These researchers concluded that substance abuse by the husband and intergenerational violence in the woman's family of origin are the most important factors differentiating wives who are abused from other women.[12]

According to the *Journal of the American Medical Association,* 16 percent of women who are battered go on to abuse alcohol, while 10 percent abuse prescription medications they were given to alleviate their stress. Several studies have shown that many women don't start drinking until after they are battered.[13] Another study determined that 85 percent of children from violent homes admitted to drinking problems that began when they were as young as eleven.[14]

Families troubled by both chemical dependency and domestic violence seem to be at greatest risk for intergenerational transmission of both problems.[15] This tendency has probably been exacerbated by the traditional reluctance to treat both problems concurrently. Also, both kinds of abuse tend to be kept as closely guarded family secrets. Shame often prevents individual family members from seeking the very help that could break the ongoing generational cycle.

The Perpetrator as a Substance Abuser

Additional research shows that abusive men with serious chemical problems are prone to abuse their partners whether drunk or sober, are violent more often, and inflict more severe injuries than abusive men without substance abuse problems. Also, substance abusers are more likely to sexually assault their partners and to be violent outside of the home.[16] Another study found that 35 percent of batterers in lesbian relationships were under the influence of chemicals at the time of the violent incidents.[17]

In Angela Browne's book, *When Battered Women Kill,* male abusers who were killed by their partners were compared to other male abusers in terms of their alcohol and drug use patterns. Drug use was found to be consistently higher among those men who were killed by their partners. Forty percent of men in the comparison group became intoxicated every day or almost every day, as opposed to 79 percent in the homicide group. Eight percent in the comparison group used street drugs every day or almost every day, compared to 30 percent in the homicide group. Even prescription drug use was significantly higher in the homicide group.[18]

The relationship between substance and domestic abuse is further complicated by differences in male and female socialization. Women who are battered while under the influence are typically blamed for the abuse. Conversely, when men abuse while under the influence, situational factors are often blamed for causing the violence. The abusive men and the women being abused *both* tend to use the male's substance abuse to explain or excuse the violence.

Many people believe in the disinhibition theory of substance abuse. As alcohol intake paralyzes the control centers in the brain, normal behavioral restraints are relaxed. Abusers rely on this theory to justify their violence and to exempt themselves from taking responsibility for their own behaviors. "Honey, if I hadn't been drunk, I would never have hit you." Since survivors have been programmed to take all of the blame, they too will excuse the abusive behavior. "I should have been less demanding, since I know what can happen when he drinks." Even society is more likely to rationalize the use of violence if chemicals are involved, and so the abuser's own statement of control is reinforced by the "internal tapes" of the survivor and the myths embraced by society.

The person being abused may also turn to chemicals as medication for the pain or simply as a survival skill. Survivors may find that using alcohol extends the calming phase or allows them to escape the horrors of the abuse by blacking out. Studies have shown that in relationships where one person is using, the other person is more likely to begin using as well. For example, abused women self-reporting the heaviest drinking patterns were in relationships with men who also abused alcohol.[19]

While much still needs to be learned about how violence is affected by various types of substance abuse, there is a general consensus that violence is frequently more severe and less predictable with the presence of drugs other than alcohol or a combination of other drugs and alcohol than with alcohol alone.[20] Also, drug responses will vary for each individual and will depend on the meanings and scripts that these individuals have associated with drug use.[21] As new drugs become available on the streets, you may need to identify new patterns of violence. For example, estimates during the first few months of 1990 showed that one-third to one-half of the individuals in drug treatment in Hawaii were being treated for ice addictions. More than 70 percent of the spousal abuse cases in Honolulu during this time involved the use of ice.[22]

Why Do People Stay in Abusive Relationships?

Immobilized by fear, many people stay in abusive relationships. They suffer from fear of reprisal from their abuser, fear of rejection by their families or churches, fear for their children, fear of harassment at their jobs, fear of letting out the family secret, or fear of their own inability to survive independently. "Research over the last ten years indicates that women who leave their batterers are at a 75 percent greater risk of being killed by the batterer than are those who stay."[23]

Many people accept their situation (and continue to take on all the blame) because they grew up with violence. Many survivors who said the words "until death do us part" feel committed to this vow. A common message abusive parents give to their married daughters who are being abused is, "You made your bed. Now lie in it." Other people stay in abusive relationships because they feel trapped. This typical response is characterized by failure to identify and address issues of domestic violence. Ironically, research has found that the most significant barrier to battered women seeking help is the typical response they receive from helping agents. Similar gatekeeping barriers have been identified for alcoholic women.[24]

Recalling individual patterns of violence may also help you understand why people stay. A client who is experiencing the calming phase of abuse may not want to think about leaving. Instead, this client may be filled with renewed hope for the future. As the tension-building phase begins again, your client may try to ignore or deny the signs. Giving up hope can be very painful. Once the tension escalates even further, your client may not have the energy to leave or may feel that leaving will be more dangerous than staying. As the violence erupts, she may no longer have the option to leave. She may be physically prevented from leaving, may become disoriented, or may be separated from the children and unwilling to leave without them. Survivors of physical and sexual abuse may be too incapacitated or too embarrassed to leave at this point. As the crisis passes, the calming phase will return, and the added use of chemicals may soothe the situation even further. Many survivors of abuse still love their abusers. The hope that things will get better may be so strong that the cycle will repeat itself again and again.

Understanding Power and Control

The balance of power and control in an abusive relationship is very clear-cut—the abuser takes it all, and the survivor gets none. To understand an abuser's insatiable need for power and control, keep in mind that abuse is a learned behavior and that most abusers were abused themselves. Because they were abused, most perpetrators have very low self-concepts and therefore feel the need to overpower and control others around them. The only model the abuser has for building his own self-esteem is to systematically break down his partner's sense of self-worth.

As shown in the following examples, an abuser may consistently take his partner's greatest self-identified strength, and hence source of self-esteem, and turn it into her greatest vulnerability. For example, each time a woman would exhibit this characteristic strength, she would be abused.[25]

Strength	*Vulnerability*	*Power and Control*
• Friendly	• Always coming on to men	• Isolation
• Helpful	• Meddling	• Emotional abuse
• Smart	• Know-it-all	• Intimidation
• Fair	• Manipulative	• Threats/coercion
• Thrifty	• Tightwad	• Economic abuse
• Feminine	• Servant	• Male privilege
• Good parent	• Overprotective	• Using the children
• Pretty	• Vain	• Physical abuse
• Attentive	• Seductive	• Sexual abuse
• Caring	• Selfish	• Minimizing, denying, blaming

In other words, the woman who prided herself on being helpful was seen by her partner as being a meddler. If her partner were working on the car and she voluntarily offered a tool, her partner would berate her for selecting the wrong tool.

If she addressed family Christmas cards, she would be reprimanded for interfering with her partner's friendships. She would consistently be punished and put down for doing what she thought was helpful. Over time, this woman's self-esteem would be stripped away to nothing. Her partner would succeed in gaining all the power and control in their relationship. The power and control wheel in Appendix A on page 31 can be a helpful tool to give your clients to help them understand the dynamics at work in an abusive relationship.

Developing Survival Skills

Individuals who are abused become very resourceful and creative in developing survival skills. Your clients may not have a conscious understanding of the dynamics of their relationship. They will not have words like *survival skills* in their vocabulary. However, they will have some almost instinctual behaviors that allow them to cope, and they may be much better at handling crises than non-crisis situations. Some of your clients' survival skills may not make any sense to you. Some of their most bizarre behaviors may be mistakenly attributed to their chemical use. In reality, these behaviors are survival skills and will persist even after sobriety is attained. Sometimes, your clients won't even consciously understand that certain "second nature" behaviors are survival skills.

As the severity and frequency of their abuse increase, your clients may need to become more creative in their survival skills. For example, if a husband normally arrives home from work at 5:00 each day, his wife may routinely pick up all the toys and send the kids to their rooms at 4:45. She does this as a preventive measure to ensure that nothing stressful will happen for her husband to use as an excuse to unleash his aggressive behavior. An outside observer would probably see nothing unusual about this woman's behavior.

In a more highly escalated situation, this man may begin brutally beating his wife. She knows that picking up the toys won't help now. Since she has no way of escaping, she begins banging her head against the wall. As she continues to abuse herself, her husband's blows stop. He stands back and laughs at her and calls her a crazy woman. While she may begin to accept the "crazy" label, she also knows that she may have just saved her own life. In this situation, an outside observer might agree that the woman has gone crazy.

The Process of Leaving

From an outsider's point of view, leaving may seem logical and simple, but the survivor probably sees things from a different perspective. While enduring the abuse may be lethal, the survivor needs to recognize leaving as a life-threatening option as well. As a chemical health professional, your support and intervention can be very important to a person trying to leave a relationship. However, the actual decisions of *if* and *when* and *how* are best left to the survivor. Of course, if you are dealing with a "vulnerable adult," you will need to be familiar with the reporting laws.

Women who decide to leave will need massive doses of support along the way. Those who decide to stay may feel excessive shame and may *assume* that you will withdraw support because they are not strong enough to leave. In many cases, making the decision to leave will take more time and require more emotional support than the actual process of leaving.

Frequently, survivors will leave the same relationship more than once. The abuser may be so convincingly remorseful during the calming phase that the survivor will agree to "give it another try." The survivor's shame and blame may draw her into returning just to see whether she could handle things differently the next time. "It is not your fault" is a message the survivor may need to hear over and over again at this stage of healing.

Chemical abuse further complicates the process of leaving. One common scenario goes like this: the survivor leaves the relationship, goes through treatment, and attains sobriety. Violence in the relationship is not addressed during chemical intervention. After treatment, the survivor tries to establish a new lifestyle but is still governed by the internalized messages that were programmed by the abuser. The abuser begins to phone, gradually increases contact, and promises a better relationship. The survivor returns to the relationship. Abuse resumes as usual. Chemical relapse occurs.

Time can also work against survivors. The longer a person is trapped in a relationship without being able to end the violence, the more likely it is that complex psychosocial problems will develop and further complicate the process of leaving. A previous history of abuse may also prolong the process.

Leaving and Grieving

Leaving may be a more emotionally painful process than the survivor had anticipated. Even though the relationship was abusive, leaving it will create a void in the survivor's life. This sense of loss will be compounded for individuals who have also gone through chemical dependency treatment. Explaining the normal phases of grieving may be helpful.

Once out of the relationship, the survivor may begin to deny or minimize the severity of the abuse. Still loving her abuser, she may cling to some denial about the finality of the separation. Admitting that she really needed to leave means giving up the hope that things might get better. All of her dreams of "living happily ever after" are shattered. The survivor may also begin to bargain with herself: "Maybe if we just separate for six months and think things over, it can still work out." or "Maybe if I exercise every day and lose ten pounds, I'll be able to have a better relationship."

When the survivor is out of imminent danger, feelings may surface that could not have been safely expressed within the relationship. Anger may be the most difficult emotion for a female survivor of abuse to handle. She has been socialized to believe that "nice girls don't get mad," and she was probably never allowed to express anger to her abuser. Substance abuse may have further dulled her feelings. Once she manages to get in touch with her anger, she may experience seemingly uncontrollable and frightening surges of rage. This will be compounded if she is also a survivor of childhood sexual abuse or of multiple abusive relationships. Your intervention skills may be needed to help her channel this rage so that she does not direct it inward. You may want to prepare her for the possibility of flashbacks and body memories and assure her that these are normal, albeit scary, parts of her healing process.

As a survivor gets in touch with her anger, she may tell you that she would like to kill her abuser or wishes that he would drop off the face of the earth. In most cases, this is a normal response to the abuse and often occurs after the woman realizes that her partner may never change and may never stop abusing her. If a survivor expresses detailed plans for how and when to kill her abuser, then you will need to act upon your statutory "duty to warn" either the potential victim or appropriate law enforcement agency.

Depression is another normal part of grieving. About 33 percent of women who remain in battering relationships suffer primary care depression. Approximately 30 percent of women who attempt suicide are battered.[26]

Survivors leave relationships with the expectation that things will be better and that the abuse will stop. In reality, the abuse may never stop but will simply take on different forms. Lacking physical access, the abuser may turn to new strategies for maintaining power and control, such as telephone harassment, court appeals, withholding financial support, drawing friends and neighbors away from the survivor, or using the children. Mounting legal fees and other financial responsibilities may seem overwhelming. Old survival skills won't necessarily work anymore, and developing new skills needed to maintain a sober, abuse-free life may seem like an impossibility. When day-to-day stresses like a clogged sink or sick child are added to the tension of the ongoing abuse, the survivor may slip into depression or chemical relapse.

The survivor's ultimate goal in terms of grieving is to reach the stage of acceptance. You may need to remind her to trust her "internal compass" and to allow herself to feel the pain in order to move beyond the pain. The healing process may be very confusing to the survivor and will be further complicated if she is also healing from substance abuse. While the healing process will vary with each individual, survivors need to know that there is no quick fix for their pain. In fact, survivors of domestic as well as chemical abuse may grieve for years into their recovery and may need to process their grief at the cognitive, emotional, psychological, and spiritual levels.[27]

Guidelines for Chemical Health Professionals

As you evaluate your role as a chemical health professional working with family violence issues, you will need to set some limits and expectations for your involvement. You have already established your expertise in the field of chemical dependency, and you cannot be expected to reach the same level of competence for all of your clients' other issues. However, the high prevalence of domestic abuse among substance abusers dictates that you have at least a baseline of knowledge about the dynamics of family violence. After reading this book alone, you will have more knowledge than many helping professionals. Unfortunately, family violence is still not a standard part of many educational training programs.

As you deal with clients in chemical dependency treatment, it is important that you expand your normal intake and assessment process to include basic questions about family violence. Your front-end validation of clients' abuse will open the door for them to begin healing. Since substance abuse and domestic abuse are both life-threatening, it is important that both issues be acknowledged as soon as they are identified. Of course, many clients will not readily admit that they are being abused, so assessment needs to be an ongoing, sometimes intuitive, process that will continue throughout treatment and often beyond.

Integrating the Assessment Process

You probably already use a formal assessment tool for chemical dependency. Your first step in integrating the assessment process would be to examine your existing tool and determine whether any of the information collected gives you insight into family violence. You likely also collect individual and family histories that may be helpful in understanding clients' behavioral patterns. For example, researchers generally agree that men who witnessed violence between their parents are three times more likely to hit their own wives than those who did not.[28]

If your present assessment tool does not provide adequate information about family violence, you can add some standard questions or develop a separate form to be administered at the same time. See Appendix B on page 32 for a sample form. It is important to ask direct and specific questions about family violence. Survivors are accustomed to concealing and minimizing the abuse and will have no difficulty evading vague questions. For example, consider the following:

"Has your partner ever hit you?"

"Yes, he punched me one time about a year ago."

This survivor is being honest and may feel very much at risk for letting out this much of the secret. However, she may be failing to mention the fact that her partner also slaps her across the room with an open hand about once a week.

A study of the interactions of emergency room physicians and their battered patients found that "the physician failed to determine the woman's relationship to her assailant in three of four interactions. In 90 percent of the interactions, the physician failed to obtain a psychosocial history, failed to ask about a history of sexual or physical abuse, failed to ask about the woman's living arrangements, and failed to address the woman's safety."[29]

In addition to the formal assessment process, you will want to gather information informally throughout the course of treatment. If you observe signs of mounting stress, you may want to explain the roller coaster analogy and watch how your client reacts to that visualization. If you notice bruises or long-sleeved turtlenecks in the middle of August, express concern and ask some specific questions. If your client finds it difficult to trust anyone, you may want to talk about the origins of that distrust.

Your goals for assessment should be to do some basic screening for family violence, to acknowledge the presence of any abuse that is discovered, and to integrate this assessment into your standard intake process for chemical dependency treatment. If there is evidence of domestic abuse, you may want to get a general impression of the nature and level of the violence by using a checklist such as the one found in Appendix B.

Tools for Protection Planning

After assessment for the presence of family violence, your greatest responsibilities to your clients are to consider their immediate safety needs, provide tools for protection planning, and make knowledgeable referrals. As a helping professional, you are responsible for facilitating the process. Your clients are responsible for their own outcomes.

Protection planning is the process of helping a survivor develop a Plan A and a Plan B before they are actually needed. The only skills required for protection planning are common sense and ingenuity. Protection planning must be very individualized, but the following ideas could be offered to help clients start thinking about what might work for them:

1. Ask neighbors to call the police whenever they hear something suspicious.
2. Hide an extra set of car and house keys.
3. Ask friends or neighbors if you can come over or call at any time of the day or night.
4. Hide enough cash for a cab or motel room.
5. File for an Order For Protection and use it.
6. Give yourself permission to call the police, and teach your children how to dial.

7. If you call the police, insist on a copy of the report and get officer badge numbers.
8. Trust your instinct and leave when you sense that the abuse is escalating.
9. Keep all important papers in one safe, accessible place (birth certificates, marriage license, insurance policies, check stubs, etc.)
10. Pack a small bag of clothes and essentials and hide it. A garbage bag will be less conspicuous than a suitcase.
11. Purchase and use a screech alarm in case you can't get to the phone.
12. Check your neighborhood for buildings open twenty-four hours and for public phones.
13. Keep a list of emergency and support numbers in a safe place, such as inside a Kotex box or in the pocket of an off-season coat.
14. Do not isolate yourself. Make daily contact with another person.
15. Build and maintain a support system for yourself.

All survivors of domestic abuse should do some protection planning. The extensiveness will vary with the severity of the abuse, and the creativity will need to increase as the sophistication and subtlety of the abuse increase. Since substance abuse may hamper a person's ability to recognize danger, the planning may change over time as your client moves from chemical dependency to sobriety.

Screening the Resources

Since many helping professionals lack training in domestic abuse, you will want to check out referrals yourself and also give your clients some tools for checking out their own contacts. Let clients know they have the right to interview therapists before committing to therapy, and, by all means, be honest about your level of expertise and comfort in dealing with family violence issues. Some suggested questions to ask before selecting a therapist or other helping professional include the following:

- *How are you qualified to work with domestic abuse?* Since few credentialed professionals have studied family violence as part of their formal education, it is important to ask about their experience of working with abuse.
- *What kind of records do you keep and what would happen if they were subpoenaed?* Even after a couple physically separates, the abuser will continue to seek power and control over the relationship and will often attempt to do so through the legal system. For example, a woman who discovers an electronic device in her telephone describes herself as "feeling paranoid." You document her feelings in your case notes, using her own terminology. Your records are subpoenaed, the woman is classified as mentally ill, and custody of children is granted to the abuser.
- *Do you believe that substance abuse causes domestic abuse?* Another way to evaluate a therapist's understanding of the dynamics of abuse is to ask for responses to didactic questions or hypothetical situations.

It is also important to recognize that traditional services may not be effective in cases involving domestic abuse. For example, after attending a support group for women with abuse issues for three weeks, one participant stated that she had learned more and felt more empowered from her brief group experience than from the previous four years she had spent in marriage counseling. Some services such as divorce mediation or family group work may actually be damaging to survivors of abuse because of the power differential between them and their abusers. The confrontation techniques traditionally used in chemical dependency treatment are also not recommended because they may be too similar to the interrogation used by abusers. Some services have real or perceived eligibility requirements that screen out people who are in need. Some clients fall through the cracks due to their financial status. One woman who called a shelter for support was simply told that she should "count her blessings" when the shelter worker heard her address!

Since each person's experience of violence is unique, after-care planning will also need to be individualized. Peer support, relevant literature, and informal resources available through friends or neighbors can be helpful along with more structured services. The availability of domestic abuse services varies from place to place. You can begin to identify the resources by talking to shelters for battered women, family violence coalitions, your local county social service department, public health department, mental health clinics, police departments, or hospital staffs. Survivors can always be directed to the resources listed in Appendix C on page 35.

Accessing the Resources

Identifying the resources is only a beginning. Many survivors of domestic abuse will have difficulty accessing services and may need advocacy to help with this process. It is not safe to assume that individuals being abused have access to the kind of communication network that most of us take for granted. Many survivors are not allowed to have a driver's license. Use of the telephone is strictly forbidden by some abusers. Other abusers may choose to live in rural locations where access to neighbors is even out of the question.

Accessing needed services may also be an overwhelming emotional task. Take the example of a woman with four young children who decides that she wants to leave her relationship. Think of the number of people that she will need to contact during the process of leaving, and try to visualize her explaining her needs to each of these people over the phone as her four children cling to her knees. Her contacts may include an advocate, her pastor, a therapist, the county social service department, the school social worker, the police, her partner's parole officer, a judge, the clerk of courts, family members, her chemical health team, her attorney, the bill collectors, a physician, and so on.

Access to some services may be indirectly controlled by the abuser. For example, women who desperately need therapy or medical attention may be unwilling to have these services reported through their insurance companies. It is safer for them to do without therapy than to let their abusers know that they are using mental health services. Third-party reimbursements for mental health services require diagnoses that might later work against survivors. In some cases, antidepressants might facilitate the healing process but are not used for fear that medical records will be subpoenaed and information will be used against the survivor.

Coordinating the Resources

There may not be enough hours in the week for your client to begin receiving all the necessary services at once. In some cases, you may be willing to assume a case management position and help your client set up a six-month plan for service delivery. Your client should be actively involved in this process so she does not become dependent on you after the initial planning is in place.

In some cases, traditional chemical dependency treatment may conflict with services geared to survivors of domestic abuse. Confidentiality is of utmost importance to a person who has been battered. The type of self-disclosure that is encouraged in Twelve Step programs may conflict with the safety needs of abuse survivors. Some aspects of the chemical dependency model may imply that survivors are to blame for their own abuse. The concept of codependency, for example, should never be applied to family violence. "If you weren't codependent, then you wouldn't have been abused." "If you weren't such a caretaker, you could have left the relationship sooner."

Survivors of both domestic and substance abuse will be making tremendous adjustments in their lives. Their healing processes will be slow, and they need to be prepared for that reality. While there is growing belief in the effectiveness of dual treatment, it is not necessary for your client to work on all existing issues with the same intensity at the same time. The important part is to *acknowledge* the presence of all the issues and then work out a manageable plan that will begin to move your client in a positive direction. The concept of One Day at a Time can be applied to healing from domestic as well as substance abuse.

Taking Care of Yourself

In order to be an effective chemical health professional, you need and deserve to take care of yourself on a personal level. You are an important person, and you do important work. You have a responsibility to nurture, rather than neglect, your own needs. Your greatest personal responsibility is to assess any unresolved issues you may have in the area of family violence and to begin your own healing if necessary. Your effectiveness as a helping professional will be compromised by these unresolved issues, and your sense of security or professional boundaries may be shaken as clients' stories trigger memories of your own abuse. You deserve to take care of yourself just as much as you would encourage others to take care of themselves.

In working with domestic abuse, you can take care of yourself by learning to network with family violence professionals. This will help you in setting appropriate limits for your involvement with clients and will allow you to listen to clients' stories without feeling responsible for having all the answers. In addition to exchanging information, you and family violence professionals can offer one another support.

Now that you understand more about the dynamics of family violence, you will see more signs of abuse than you ever noticed before. You may recall a client who you worked with a year ago and now realize that domestic abuse was the missing piece of the puzzle that didn't make sense. As you work with more survivors of domestic abuse, you will become more intuitive and more comfortable in asking questions.

As clients begin to trust your understanding of family violence, they will share more. You will hear of atrocities and human suffering that may be overwhelming. Again, you need to take care of yourself and ask for support when needed.

Your new knowledge of family violence will make your job easier because acknowledging the domestic abuse will increase the likelihood that chemical dependency treatment will work and that sobriety will be maintained. In addition, you will find new challenges. As you continue to integrate the assessment and intervention processes, you will learn and grow and discover more about the complex interconnections between substance abuse and family violence.

APPENDIX A

POWER AND CONTROL

USING COERCION AND THREATS — Making and/or carrying out threats to do something to hurt her • threatening to leave her, to commit suicide, to report her to welfare • making her drop charges • making her do illegal things.

USING INTIMIDATION — Making her afraid by using looks, actions, gestures • smashing things • destroying her property • abusing pets • displaying weapons.

USING EMOTIONAL ABUSE — Putting her down • making her feel bad about herself • calling her names • making her think she's crazy • playing mind games • humiliating her • making her feel guilty.

USING ISOLATION — Controlling what she does, who she sees and talks to, what she reads, where she goes • limiting her outside involvement • using jealously to justify actions.

MINIMIZING, DENYING AND BLAMING — Making light of the abuse and not taking her concerns about it seriously • saying the abuse didn't happen • shifting responsibility for abusive behavior • saying she caused it.

USING CHILDREN — Making her guilty about the children • using the children to relay messages • using visitation to harass her • threatening to take the children away.

USING MALE PRIVILEGE — Treating her like a servant • making all the big decisions • acting like the "master of the castle" • being the one to define men's and women's roles.

USING ECONOMIC ABUSE — Preventing her from getting or keeping a job • making her ask for money • giving her an allowance • taking her money • not letting her know about or have access to family income.

Reprinted with permission of
DOMESTIC ABUSE INTERVENTION PROJECT
206 West Fourth Street
Duluth, Minnesota 55806
218-722-4134

APPENDIX B

Assessment of Domestic Abuse

Instructions: This assessment may be completed by a client in the presence of a support person or may be used as an interview tool. Part I may be used early in intervention to gain a general impression of a client's experience, while Part II further specifies the nature and extent of abuse. Part II may be used as an educational tool to define abuse or as a personal inventory to understand individual patterns of abuse. The major headings in Part II may be used as a quick screening device, while the complete checklist may be used repetitively as clients increase their understanding of abuse and regain memories.

I. Name _____ Date _____

Relationship to abuser _____ Abuser's gender _____

Define "domestic abuse" in your own words

Briefly describe first abusive incident _____

month   year

Briefly describe most recent incident _____

month   year

List other (previous or current) abusive relationships.

II. Use an "X" to indicate abuse during the past six months and an "*" for abuse occurring more than six months ago.

DID YOUR ABUSER:

A. Use Intimidation
1. ___ Frighten by words/actions
2. ___ Smash/destroy property
3. ___ Harm/endanger pets
4. ___ Display weapons
5. ___ Scream/swear at you
6. ___ Sway others to doubt you
7. _____

B. Use emotional abuse
1. ___ Ridicule/humiliate you
2. ___ Use name-calling
3. ___ Play mind games
4. ___ Always criticize you
5. ___ Withhold approval/affection
6. ___ Lead children to abuse you
7. _____

C. Use children
1. ___ Put children "in the middle"
2. ___ Use visitation to harass you
3. ___ Threaten to take/kidnap kids

4. ___ Abuse you in front of children
5. ___ Punish kids for your "mistakes"
6. _____

D. Use "male privilege"
1. ___ Treat you like a slave
2. ___ Control family decisions
3. ___ Enforce stereotypical male/female roles and privileges
4. ___ Use Scripture against you
5. ___ Abuse you in front of other male friends
6. _____

E. Use economic abuse
1. ___ Refuse to work
2. ___ Keep you from working
3. ___ Control all spending money
4. ___ Hide checkbook/credit cards
5. ___ Refuse to pay medical bills
6. ___ Take back gifts
7. ___ Prolong legal procedures
8. _____

F. Use isolation

1. __ Control activities/ relationships
2. __ Control phone use
3. __ Forbid you to drive
4. __ Not socialize with you
5. __ Act out at family events
6. _____

G. Minimize, deny, and blame

1. __ Disregard the abuse
2. __ Say how lucky you are
3. __ Deny responsibility for behavior
4. __ Blame/shame you
5. __ Blame your family
6. _____

H. Use coercion and threats

1. __ Threaten to harm you
2. __ Threaten children/ family
3. __ Break your confidences
4. __ Threaten suicide

5. __ Coerce you to drop charges
6. __ Coerce you to abuse children
7. _____

I. Use sexual violence

1. __ Ridicule your body parts
2. __ Accuse you of affairs
3. __ Force sex/affection
4. __ Withhold sex/affection
5. __ Berate you for previous relationships
6. __ Control how you dress
7. _____

J. Use physical abuse⁺

1. __ Physically strike you
2. __ Deprive you of food/ sleep
3. __ Harass you to the point of physical illness
4. __ Drive recklessly
5. __ Lock you out or abandon you
6. __ Prevent medical care
7. _____

⁺Primary categories from "Power and Control Wheel," Domestic Abuse Intervention Project, Duluth, MN (see Appendix A).

APPENDIX C

Resources

NATIONAL COALITION
AGAINST DOMESTIC
VIOLENCE
P.O. Box 34102
Washington, D.C. 20043-4103
202-638-6388
National network of safe
houses, shelters, and counseling

MICHIGAN COALITION
AGAINST DOMESTIC
VIOLENCE
1-800-333-SAFE
1-800-873-6363 for hearing
impaired
National 24-hour crisis line

Endnotes

1. Kurt Anderson, "Private Violence," *Time* (Sept. 5, 1983): 23.

2. "Domestic Violence Begets Other Problems of Which Physicians Must Be Aware to Be Effective," *The Journal of the American Medical Association* 264, no. 8 (Aug. 22/29, 1990): 943.

3. Pamela Weinberger, "Domestic Violence: When Love Hurts," *The Lion* (May 1988): 6.

4. Richard J. Gelles and Murray A. Straus, *Intimate Violence* (New York: Simon and Schuster, 1988), 104.

5. "Domestic Violence Begets Other Problems," 943.

6. Beth Gorney, "Domestic Violence and Chemical Dependency: Dual Problems, Dual Interventions," *Journal of Psychoactive Drugs* 2, no. 2 (Apr.-June 1989): 130.

7. Beverly Rainbolt and Michael Greene, *Behind the Veil of Silence* (Center City, Minn.: Hazelden Educational Materials, 1990), 10.

8. Gorney, 230.

9. Gelles and Straus, 121.

10. Gelles and Straus, 91.

11. N. Ann Lowrance, "Domestic Violence," in *Women: Alcohol and Other Drugs,* ed. Ruth C. Engs (Alcohol and Drug Problems Association), 171.

12. Glenda Kaufman Kantor and Murray A. Straus, "Substance Abuse as a Precipitant of Wife Abuse Victimizations," *American Journal of Drug and Alcohol Abuse* 15 no. 2 (1989): 186.

13. "Domestic Violence Begets Other Problems," 943.

14. Lowrance, 171.

15. Gorney, 232.

16. Angela Browne, *When Battered Women Kill* (New York: The Free Press, 1987), 73.

17. Lowrance, 170.

18. Browne, 71.

19. Lowrance, 171.

20. Gorney, 230-31.

21. Kaufman Kantor and Straus, 184.

22. Paul McEnroe, "Hawaii is Fighting Losing Battle Against the Popularity of Drug 'Ice'," *Minneapolis Star Tribune* (May 18, 1990).

23. Lowrance, 168.

24. Lowrance, 170.

25. Ginny NiCarthy, Karen Merriam, and Sandra Coffman, *Talking It Out: A Guide to Groups for Abused Women* (Seattle, Wash.: Seal Press, 1984), 105-9.

26. "Domestic Violence Begets Other Problems," 943; Lowrance, 168.

27. Susan Schaefer and Sue Evans, *Women, Sexuality and the Process of Recovery* (Minneapolis: Haworth Press, 1987), 108.

28. Gorney, 232.

29. "Domestic Violence Intervention Calls for More Than Treating Injuries," *The Journal of the American Medical Association:* 264 no. 8 (Aug. 22-29, 1990): 939.

Suggested Reading

Browne, Angela. *When Battered Women Kill.* New York: The Free Press, 1987.

Fedders, Charlotte, and Laura Elliot. *Shattered Dreams.* New York: Harper & Row, 1987.

Gelles, Richard J., and Murray A. Straus. *Intimate Violence.* New York: Simon and Schuster, 1988.

NiCarthy, Ginny. *Getting Free.* Seattle, Wash.: Seal Press, 1982.

NiCarthy, Ginny. *The Ones Who Got Away.* Seattle, Wash.: Seal Press, 1987.

NiCarthy, Ginny, Karen Merriam, and Sandra Coffman. *Talking It Out: A Guide to Groups for Abused Women.* Seattle, Wash.: Seal Press, 1984.

Rainbolt, Beverly, and Michael Greene. *Behind the Veil of Silence: Family Violence and Alcohol Abuse.* Center City, Minn.: Hazelden Educational Materials, 1990.

Switzer, M'liss Mary (Bock), and Katherine Hale. *Called to Account.* St. Paul: 1777 Sheridan Avenue, St. Paul, MN 55116, 1984.

Walker, Lenore. *Terrifying Love.* New York: Harper & Row, 1989.

Walker, Lenore. *The Battered Woman.* New York: Harper & Row, 1979.

PART II

Dealing with Childhood Sexual Abuse in Treatment

Kristin Kunzman

This section of the book will help familiarize you with the basics of recognizing and dealing with women clients who have a history of childhood sexual abuse. You have probably learned that many of your chemically dependent female clients were sexually, physically, or verbally abused as children. Or they may have suffered all these forms of abuse. There is also a growing recognition that the number of male children abused is much greater than previously thought. We are aware that many of the problems stemming from abuse and the methods for healing from it are the same for men and women. But there are differences, and since my knowledge comes from working with women, the information presented here is addressed to their healing.

Studies and surveys show that as many as 60-70 percent of women in chemical dependency treatment have been sexually abused or assaulted before age eighteen.[1]

Statistics further show that a primary caregiver or parent is chemically dependent in 39-65 percent of families in which childhood sexual abuse occurs.[2] When chemical dependency and sexual abuse coexist in a family, you can also find these basic dynamics:

- denial
- secrets
- getting needs met through alcohol or other drugs rather than healthy relationships
- lack of nurturing
- inability to express understanding or feelings
- feelings of neglect and abandonment

When there is chemical dependency in a family, the framework for isolating and keeping secrets from the outside world is already in place; the sexual abuse becomes just another secret. Chemical dependency is prevalent in the lives of survivors of childhood abuse. Many begin using chemicals, like other addictive or compulsive behaviors, as a way to dull the pain of the abuse and block out any of the horrible memories.

Approximately one woman in three reports having been sexually abused before the age of eighteen.[3]

Although there is no easy answer to the link between abuse and chemical dependency, we do know that many abuse survivors used alcohol and other drugs to repress memories of their abuse and that many survivors suffer from extremely low self-esteem without having any idea of where this feeling comes from. This syndrome is tailor-made for anyone with the slightest tendency toward substance abuse. Because of this complex picture, many survivors of childhood sexual abuse become addicted and eventually find their way to chemical dependency treatment.

As memories of their childhood abuse are no longer being repressed by chemicals, some of your newly sober clients may be flooded by strange and frightening feelings. For most survivors, however, memories of the abuse resurface only after years of sobriety. Few women enter treatment fully and painfully aware of their sexual abuse history, and some women enter treatment with absolutely no recollection of their abuse.

It is important for you to understand what a sexually abused survivor may be feeling and how you can best help her during treatment. Many women have kept the secret of their abuse throughout their years of chemical use. Even women who fully remember their abuse may have never revealed their history to anyone. The treatment setting may be the first time they hear information about sexual abuse and its connection with their chemical dependency. It is a crucial point for some and you can play an important role.

Your having some knowledge about childhood abuse can help maximize your clients' trust in you. It can also help you understand the complex interplay between histories of childhood abuse and substance abuse. Further, it will help you make better aftercare referrals. In aftercare, when there is additional help from the proper specialists and/or a strong support group, childhood abuse survivors can more fully deal with the aftermath of their abuse as a problem separate from, yet connected to, their addiction.

What Is Childhood Sexual Abuse And How Does It Affect Victims?

Childhood sexual abuse is

- a physical violation of a child's body through any sort of sexual contact.
- a psychological violation of a child through verbal or visual sexual behavior.

In either case, abuse is neglectful, disrespectful, and hurtful because it violates a child's basic rights to be protected, nurtured, and guided. Childhood sexual abuse, no matter what form it takes, inflicts great and long-lasting hurt on its victims.

It doesn't matter whether the abuse was physical, verbal, or visual. It may have consisted of

- touching genitals (child being sexually touched or sexually touching an adult or older child).
- fondling.
- pornography shown to children.
- embarrassing and degrading sexual remarks or looks.
- exhibitionism.

In a family where sexual abuse occurs, the typical dynamics of poor personal boundaries, parents who lacked good parenting role models for themselves, inability to nurture family members consistently, and lack of generational boundaries all add up to uneven care and mistreatment of children. Many of these families may have several types of abuse and mistreatment going on at the same time, including the following:

- Physical Abuse—This can include hitting, shoving, kicking, or unusual and severe punishment.
- Physical Neglect—Some families do not provide adequate food, clothing, or shelter for family members.
- Emotional Neglect—Some family members withhold emotional care (verbal and physical affection) from one another and especially from the children.

- Chemically Dependent Parents—Much of the time, practicing alcoholics or other addicts are emotionally absent from their children and spouses. This is a result of the nature of their altered moods and preoccupation with drugs. They may be verbally, physically, and emotionally abusive as well as sexually abusive. At best, alcoholic parents are inconsistent in their behavior, leaving children feeling unsafe, unloved, and somehow responsible for the abuse or neglect.
- Verbal Abuse—This can vary from subtle to vicious, but whatever form it takes may land harsh emotional blows to children and teens. When a child is ridiculed, called names, or made to feel unworthy and defective by verbal shaming, there may be long-term hurtful effects similar to those of physical abuse. Extreme efforts to control every aspect of a child's behavior violates children's rights and is non-nurturing.

The Cycle of Abuse

There are cultural issues that perpetuate the cycle of abuse from one generation to the next. For example, most sex offenders were themselves abused as children and are typically male. Since our culture encourages boys to be tough and not victims, it discourages sexually abused boys from talking about their abuse. Many never receive any help in dealing with their feelings. And a significant number may later turn to abusing others.

Bear in mind, however, that most abused men and women do not themselves become abusers. But for many, the cycle of abuse leaves them open to forming abusive relationships.

Families Where Abuse Takes Place

Undernurturing families where serious abuse or neglect occurs share similarities. These include violations of family members' basic rights to be protected, cared for, and not violated in any way—including physically, verbally, emotionally, or sexually. Some of the most common similarities may remind you of the typical alcoholic family system. Some of what you teach your clients about the effects of drug abuse—theirs or their parents'—will also be important information that helps them understand the effects of their childhood abuse.

Boundaries Are Not Respected

Boundaries that allow developing children to feel competent, safe, in charge, and to trust their perceptions of the world often don't exist in families where either chemical dependency or childhood abuse takes place. The physical, verbal, or psychological violation of these boundaries is probably the primary source of a child's pain. In addiction, there is usually no modeling of healthy boundaries by the adults. Children are not encouraged to have boundaries and those they have are regularly invaded by various combinations of verbal, physical, sexual, and psychological abuse.

Some people who were sexually abused may have only gotten attention during the abuse, and as a result learned that validation and abuse go hand in hand. Others may have sought security by trying to become "invisible." Both of these situations are distorted extremes of healthy boundaries and produce the same unhealthy effects. Most families where there is abuse and chemical dependency swing from being overly involved in one situation to virtually ignoring a child or being very disengaged in another. The common denominator is that the child is not respected as a developing individual with the right to respect and protection. Adults who grew up looking for safety in these families will also often fall into one of these extremes or swing back and forth between them.

Unskilled Parents and Role Reversals

These adults are poor at identifying their own needs or asking their partners for anything. Most likely they also came from undernurturing families and didn't learn healthy ways of getting their needs fulfilled—it wasn't modeled for them by *their* parents, and so it becomes a multigenerational problem. They also are usually uncomfortable and inexperienced in expressing their feelings. Consequently, as spouses, they may develop a poor system for caring for one another and getting care in return. In a home where abuse takes place—just as in a home where one or both parents are alcoholic—the parents may have looked to the children to get their needs met. A child may become a helper, confidante, a parent to younger siblings, or a sexual partner.

The Secret of Abuse and Family Isolation

Because they have difficulty sharing their feelings, these parents often don't have close friends outside the family. Many undernurturing families where abuse occurs may look good to those in their communities, as do many families that include an alcoholic parent. They may even be quite active within that community, but their home life is a secret, and they usually remain isolated from others. This isolation increases the tendency to treat children as adults. Therefore, adult survivors often feel very guilty if they stop being their mom's or dad's confidante, and they may feel disloyal talking about family secrets, such as the child abuse or the drug use.

Siblings are often competitive with one another for their parents' affection. They seldom feel safe or free of worries long enough to be children and play. They seem to feel that if one of them is getting attention, there will not be any left for the rest. At other times, siblings may give more parenting to younger siblings and run interference of abuse. The undernurtured needs of these children make them easy prey to sexual abusers both inside and outside the family.

How Abuse Affects Survivors

Childhood sexual abuse affects survivors in many ways that they carry into adulthood. Some of these effects may sound similar to patterns also common to newly recovering alcoholics, such as shame, low self-esteem, isolation, difficulty trusting others, and minimizing. For survivors of childhood abuse, these issues go back to early childhood—when they were betrayed and starved for love by the very people they were supposed to count on. Abuse survivors who are drug-dependent have usually been isolated all of their lives. The intensity of their shame, their difficulty in trusting, and their feelings of isolation are indicators that these feelings probably predate their abuse of alcohol and other drugs. Very often, a person who has been sexually abused as a child may also suffer from post-traumatic stress disorder. This may not be the perfect diagnosis for people who have been abused, but it gets at some major symptoms and emphasizes the seriousness of their trauma.[4]

Post-Traumatic Stress Disorder

This disorder suggests that survivors experienced something in their childhood so intense and out of the ordinary that it is still affecting them as adults. The following symptoms are listed in the DSM-III-R :[5]

- The person has experienced an event that is outside the range of usual human experience and that would be markedly distressing to almost anyone, such as serious threats to her life or physical well-being.
- The traumatic event is persistently re-experienced in the form of intrusive thoughts, recurrent dreams, flashbacks, and intense psychological distress during exposure to events that symbolize aspects of the original traumatic event.
- Symptoms include persistent avoidance of stimuli associated with the trauma, numbing of general responsiveness, efforts to avoid thoughts of the trauma, inability to recall important aspects of the trauma, diminished interest in life, feelings of detachment from others, restricted range of affect, and the sense of a foreshortened future.

- Persistent symptoms of increased arousal are also very often present. These can include difficulty falling or staying asleep, irritability, anger outbursts, difficulty concentrating, hypervigilance, and exaggerated startle responses.

People who were sexually abused as children and are chemically dependent likely have used chemicals to medicate feelings, to avoid frightening thoughts, and/or to minimize chances of recalling aspects of the abuse trauma. Women survivors who suffer from symptoms of post-traumatic stress disorder may be especially fearful of being hurt or victimized and tend to dissociate or "tune out." Their habits of staying distant or detached prevent them from effectively joining in treatment groups. Sometimes it helps to redirect them back to the group through a less threatening issue another member has shared—but that they can still relate to. This may help them better concentrate and counteract their desire to tune out. Giving them feedback that helps them identify and connect with others can usually help them overcome some of their detachment. Encouraging them to think of what would help them feel safer in group or individual sessions can help them feel more in charge of their safety.

Women survivors of sexual abuse may suffer from

- *Confusion of Sex and Affection; Confusing Lovers with Abusers (Flashbacks).* The only time many survivors got attention was during the times they were abused. This creates confusion and sets them up to get their emotional needs met through being sexual. Being sexual may have been the only way they felt they had any value or power, and they may have bartered being sexual for clothes, presents, favors, or to spare younger siblings from abuse. These patterns may continue into adulthood, and such superficial sexual encounters may lead survivors to feel even more shameful and responsible for their abuse.

Survivors who remember any of their abuse may find it is so interwoven with their sexuality that when they try to be sexual, even with a loving partner, it sets off a flashback from a certain touch, gesture, sight, or sound. Before treatment they may have used alcohol or other drugs to suppress these effects. Recovering survivors who remember no abuse may find that sobriety, without the repressive effects of drugs, can actually bring on flashbacks for the first time in their lives. As one survivor put it: "I always knew I used to run away from something that terrified me and made me sick when a man touched me, but it wasn't until I sobered up that I finally realized I was running from sexual abuse by my oldest brother."

- *Repression, Dissociation, Personality Splits.* These are the hall-marks of childhood sexual abuse survivors. Repression or selective amnesia covering years of their early life indicates intense trauma. Dissociating—sometimes referred to as *spacing out*—is a common coping mechanism that children use to "take themselves away" when the abuse is happening. It often continues into adulthood as a coping mechanism. The most extreme form of dissociating, and one seldom seen, is the forming of multiple personalities. The National Association of Multiple Personality Disorders reported in 1989 that almost all of the studied individuals with multiple personalities were usually severely and cruelly sexually abused.

- *Distorted Body Image.* Because abused children very often believe the abuse was their fault, many survivors have long-term feelings of self-hatred toward their bodies. This is especially true if they responded at all to the sexual touches— a common and natural response. Another way their body images get distorted is by the type of attention the abuser gave them, or by which parts of their body the abuser may have touched or remarked about. They may then feel par-ticularly disgusted by those body parts. Many survivors develop eating disorders. Some may try to protect them-selves from sexual advances by being extremely thin and not looking sexual. Other survivors may soothe themselves with food or add layers of fat for protection—again, trying not to look sexual to potential abusers.

- *Lack of Self-Respect.* The most damaging effect of childhood sexual abuse is the invasiveness of the abuse and lack of respect for the child's body and person. It is imperative that survivors learn about setting limits for how they treat others and how they allow others to treat them. In your sessions and groups, you can help survivors by modeling and setting boundaries that protect them.

Guidelines for Therapists

As previously indicated, many of the women in treatment who have been victims of childhood sexual abuse will either be only dimly aware of the abuse, or aware but unwilling to talk about it. Therefore, you can help them by offering general information about abuse (the dynamics of families where abuse happens, aftereffects of abuse, how to get help, etc.) either to them as a group (which may include men), or in a women's group specifically devoted to women's issues. Some techniques used by chemical dependency counselors may be confrontational and counterproductive for clients who are survivors of childhood abuse. Historically, confrontation was an important cornerstone of chemical dependency treatment programs—to help addicted people break through their denial. It is still important to be able to gently push them to look at an issue when you think they are ready. But it is important to maintain a fine balance between pushing and being supportive by providing information and understanding that nudge women survivors along.

Survivors who are extremely shameful may take even gentle pushing and feedback as confirmation of "what a bad person I am." When survivors feel shameful and either can't or won't hear what you say, they may shut you out in the same manner they shut out their abuse when experiencing it. Anything that mimics the abuse dynamics can trigger in them a defense mechanism or bring on intense feelings of shame. You can help them avoid this by paying attention to signs that a client has "spaced out" from being involved. This can include the client's eyes glazing over, lack of eye contact, head down, a feeling she is not listening, and incongruent responses to what you have just said. When this happens, ask her where she is and what she has heard you say. You need to be concerned that you are either discussing a topic she is not ready to discuss or that she may have reacted negatively to something you said.

You can guide abuse survivors to literature, support groups, and other professionals who deal with recovery from childhood sexual abuse. Women survivors in treatment can feel very hopeless and may think they have two awful problems that seem insurmountable. You can encourage them by letting them know that many people have histories of chemical abuse and sexual abuse—and that many have overcome these problems. It will be an important step for them to see there is a connection between their abuse and their drug dependency. It is also important for them to know they need not be alone in struggling with these problems. When they begin to understand how all their issues interact, they are less likely to be overwhelmed. Instead, they can have hope that both recoveries go hand in hand and may be worked on at the same time.

Building Effective Boundaries with Clients

As professionals, we can most effectively teach others to have good boundaries by modeling good boundaries ourselves, monitoring theirs, and openly talking about the rules and boundaries that are operating in group or individual therapy.

For example, it is important not to unduly press these survivors for information about their abuse. Instead, try to follow their pace, and move at a speed comfortable to the particular woman. Let her know why and how you are doing this. Many survivors have never had boundaries—never had their rights respected—and do not even know when those rights are trespassed. Make it clear to your client that you respect her rights and want her to tell you when it seems you are moving too fast or if she feels uncomfortable. This educates a survivor to the fact that she *does* have rights. What you accomplish in your interactions has more impact than anything you can say.

51

Encourage survivors to set boundaries, and help monitor them. Survivors of abuse may answer every question anybody asks them, no matter how personal, then later feel they said more than they wanted to. You may be the first person she has ever talked to about the abuse. She may want to tell it all and even then may be telling only what she remembers or thinks you want to hear. Let her know that she needs to tell you when she feel uncomfortable talking about something. If you suspect that someone is saying too much all at once, slow her down and ask her if it feels okay to be telling so much. You will usually know that she is saying too much when her emotions seem unusually intense, she seems extremely uncomfortable, or she cannot maintain eye contact. This may mean she feels overloaded or very shameful. When people are not ready to tell so much, they can become scared to open up later because they feel too exposed and out of control.

While allowing for flexibility, set your own limits with clients. For example, women survivors need to know that even professionals cannot be available all the time—that you must have time boundaries, topic boundaries about personal questions, and routine professional-client boundaries. The professional-client boundary can sometimes be difficult for professionals, especially when the professional has strong feelings about a woman's story of abuse—while the woman shows no affect. Even though it is empathic for you to express strong feelings for clients who express none, your intense reaction may scare them if they haven't asked you what you think. There certainly are times when it is appropriate to tell women that you have strong feelings from listening to their experiences, that you find it very sad that some children and teens go through such abuse. But the woman needs to be asked or needs to let you know if she wants to hear your reactions. It is also important to realize that if your feelings are too intense, her story may be tapping into some of your own feelings. If so, you will need to investigate why. If you have unresolved feelings about abuse in your background, you may not be the best counselor for another abuse survivor.

It will be helpful to ask women survivors to look at the ways their boundaries may have been invaded or damaged by family interactions, and how they were specifically treated. Once they begin to think of boundaries as tangible and are aware of how they were disregarded or violated, clients can begin the healing and rebuilding stage. Many people whose boundaries were violated avoid closeness to protect themselves from being hurt again. Learning about boundaries will make it easier for clients to trust and understand how they can be protected and still get closer to others.

Intakes and Interviewing

Most intake interviews consist of a client's family history, health history, and drug history. Remember, though, people may not yet trust enough to give extremely personal information about themselves. For that matter, they may be unclear whether there *was* alcoholism or abuse in their families. In any case, their denial will probably be high when they are first entering treatment; they may feel shameful and protective of their families. This is the main reason that statistics on abuse, alcoholism, or family violence are not very accurate when collected from people just entering treatment. Such statistics vary so much, depending on when they were taken, in what type of program, and whether in primary treatment or aftercare.

You may ask questions about childhood abuse during this history. Victims may not recognize what happened to them as abuse—especially if the abuse did not involve any touching, but instead was in the form of sexual remarks, sexual looks, or exhibitionism. Begin by explaining nonthreatening examples of abuse—both touching and not touching. Approach the subject in a general way, asking for no details. To make it seem routine, yet not insensitive, begin the client's family history by adding that it is very common for people in chemical dependency treatment to have a family history of alcoholism and/or abuse—sexual, physical, or verbal. This is a place to begin validating the idea that if she has this dual history, she will probably need to talk about it—to the extent she is comfortable talking about it—while in treatment. Otherwise, feelings surrounding any abuse may prevent her from feeling good about herself. Ask her about how it felt to grow up in her family. Was there any hitting or name-calling? Were there sexual remarks or any sexual touches?

- What to do when clients answer yes to questions about childhood sexual abuse:
    - When clients answer yes with no emotion, let them know they may have feelings about the abuse that they'll need to talk about when they're ready.
    - If clients burst forth with many feelings and details, respectfully slow them down and affirm their feelings. Some clients may pour out all their feelings even though they don't know you and aren't ready. Later, they may feel shameful and scared. Let them know that it would be helpful for them to work with a sexual abuse specialist, that you can talk more about these issues throughout their treatment, and that their abuse will be an area in which you will give them some help with aftercare suggestions.
    - If a woman answers no, but you suspect there may be a history of abuse, let it go until a time when it may come up again, perhaps after a lecture on the topic. This is not a time to push, since it may terrify her and actually interfere with her ability to share her history. It is common at this point to hear abuse survivors speak of their close families and of fond childhood memories. If their childhood sounds too perfect, that may be an indication of childhood trauma. A client who can't remember much of her childhood or who has large memory blanks may also be repressing memories of childhood abuse. This is especially true of lack of memories for the years after age six—older-grade school days and teens.
    - It is usually not helpful to push for details of the abuse. That will feel very intrusive to clients, yet they may be unable to set boundaries and to refuse to say more. You

need to monitor those boundaries for them to avoid re-creating feelings of intrusion and abuse.

- How to understand the signs that someone may have been abused:
    - Lack of emotion as clients talk about their childhood. Many chemically dependent people have repressed their feelings through use of chemicals, and it is common that they will display fewer feelings in treatment, especially in the beginning. When their lack of emotional response is extreme, it may be a clue that they disconnected or dissociated from their feelings for some reason. Children dissociate from feelings surrounding traumatic events, not happy ones.
    - The client can't remember much about childhood. The longer some survivors are sober, the more likely they are to regain memories of the abuse. Many recovering women in aftercare mention that their inventories or Fifth Steps taken in treatment were just the tip of the iceberg—because that was all they could remember. Or they didn't see their past abuse as harmful to themselves or others. Yet when a client talks about having no memory of her life after age six or eight (when almost all people have some memory), it is almost a given that she suffers from a form of severe trauma (abuse)—and by suppressing the memory, she has protected herself from the trauma.
    - Many sexual partners and superficial sexual encounters. This is a common response for survivors of abuse. They come to see they have power or are valued as sexual people. For many, this is a way to be close and get some nurturing without being so vulnerable with another person, without sharing their thoughts and emotions. Others will continue to have many sexual partners as a way to master or undo the abuse and feel more powerful.[6] Drugs lower inhibitions and "protect" such clients from being vulnerable by providing an insulating effect.

However, drugs tend to perpetuate this behavior of having many sexual encounters.

- Someone whose actions are seductive or flirtatious. Women who continually act flirtatious and dress and act seductively are likely candidates for histories of sexual abuse. They were conditioned to be sexual to get attention and acceptance.

- Lack of healthy boundaries. There will be women survivors who either lack boundaries because they were never allowed to have any or who have extremely rigid boundaries to protect themselves. The former will have a tendency to tell all and not protect themselves; the latter will be so well defended that it will be hard to connect with them. (Healthy boundaries keep out hurtful people and abusive behaviors, but let in nurturing, respectful people and behaviors.)

- Self-hate and extremely low self-esteem. Low self-esteem can be seen among the whole population of chemically dependent persons. When people with low self-esteem display an intense self-hatred and self-blame, the roots may lie in childhood sexual abuse. Be particularly attuned to the clients who intentionally cut themselves or inflict other self-abuse. Cutting behavior is almost exclusively connected to people with histories of sexual abuse and other forms of cruelty. Their actions are a way to perpetuate their abuse and thus stay "loyal" to their families. In some cases these survivors are trying to send a message of how much they hurt inside. In effect, they try to match up the outside pain with their inside pain. Another reason they may do it is to relieve tension. Most treatment centers have clients sign release forms so they can obtain records for clients' previous counseling and mental health hospitalizations. But you may not have the records by intake time, and clients may feel too uncomfortable sharing that information so soon.

- The client has members in her family of origin who are chemically dependent. This does not automatically mean she has been sexually abused, but it does raise the odds. When caregiving adults are preoccupied with drugs and other survival issues, the family's children are sure to be emotionally neglected and likely to seek attention elsewhere. This makes them more vulnerable to sexual abuse outside the family from neighbors, family friends, babysitters, and so forth, as well as from inside the family, such as from parents or from other siblings who also are not getting their needs met.

Effective Ways to Counsel Survivors

Believe your clients—people don't make up these painful histories.

*   *Be compassionate, but do not have their feelings for them.* On the one hand, it is important that you express your feelings to them about the abuse, so that you are not seen as one more person who does not care. On the other hand, it is important that your feelings be tempered and that they not be presented so strongly that their intensity scares off the survivors before they are able to be in touch with their own feelings.
*   *Assure clients that they will remember what they need to remember to heal themselves.* Let them know that they do not have to remember every detail of their childhood. When they are ready, they will remember as much as necessary to heal. Repressed memories come back in bits and pieces: a feeling, an image, or a physical sensation. The process is different for each survivor.
*   *Be very patient.* Don't confront or challenge survivors without presenting options. Encourage them to take your voiced feelings or comments as feedback, so they can think about what you say and see if it fits for them. Don't present your thoughts as a judgment, or clients may feel it as more abuse. If that happens, they are liable to dissociate and hear nothing more.

- *Avoid being aggressive or confrontational in sessions.* Confrontation can inhibit your ability to build trust, and it can feel shaming to women survivors—even when you are discussing their chemical use and not their history of abuse.
- *These women need supportive therapy.* This doesn't mean you enable or excuse them, but it does mean you are supportive. Look for signs that they feel shamed by your feedback, because they are used to interpreting what they hear through a "shame filter." If you are not sure how they felt about something you said, be sure you check it out with them.
- *Orient survivors to the present when you suspect they are dissociating or feeling re-traumatized.* Occasionally, as women survivors are retelling a memory about their abuse, they may actually slip into a state of re-experiencing the abuse. The likelihood of this happening is minimal—but it may happen. This state of reliving the abuse means a woman has slipped into a trance state and become that five- or six-year-old who was abused. The person may cry, talk differently, or not talk at all. In a situation like this, it will be important that you talk calmly to her and reorient her back to the room and the present. While it is important for most women to remember some of their repressed memories, it is also important that they do not become re-traumatized by actually reliving the experiences. Survivors who experience this extreme form of dissociating will need to be referred to a specialist, psychologist, psychiatrist, or other team member who covers this area.

All survivors can benefit from hearing and understanding that distancing and emotional "going away" are common survivor skills that protected them as children. Remind them that they are adults now and are only *remembering* their experiences. The events are not happening now—their younger selves can never be abused again. Have them say their names and state where they are. This distinction between the past and present is important and will spare recovering survivors much pain and terror. Extreme dissociating is unusual, but it is common for survivors to dissociate in less dramatic ways. It may be a time when you feel they are not listening, are looking out the window, or are otherwise uninvolved. Tell them it feels as if they are not there and ask them if they need distance. Validate for them that it is probably a difficult topic and say you can move on to something else if they prefer.

Helpful Information For Abuse Survivors in Treatment

Women who are recovering from both substance abuse and childhood sexual abuse tend to be quite hopeless about actually believing their lives can change. Following are some thoughts about recovery that can help them to start believing they can have a worthwhile future.

They Are Not Alone

It is common for people who suffered childhood sexual abuse to use chemicals to cope, and this can lead to addiction. It can be comforting for them to know that the abuse didn't happen because they were defective or in some way caused it themselves, but to know that, unfortunately, many children are sexually abused. It can also reduce shame to know that using chemicals was a coping method and may even have served them well for a time.

People Do Heal from Childhood Abuse

Healing can be a long process, and they need to trust that with help, they will progress at their own pace. They can't do everything at once, nor do they need to remember everything from their past. Some survivors may need to write in a journal or tell an abuse specialist about every incident they remember. Others need only to tell one incident that communicates to another person what they went through. Still others, a very small percentage, may feel their abuse is resolved or isn't anything that needs resolution.

It Is Not Their Fault

Most abuse survivors feel responsible in some way for their abuse. It is very helpful for them to know that other people recognize that what happened to them was terribly wrong and not their fault. It may take them many years to truly believe that, but information about *why* the abuse was not their fault is an important part of helping them internalize that belief. You can tell them that children and young teens are *never* responsible for sexual contact with an older adolescent or an adult.

It can be helpful to ask them why they feel so responsible. It aids the process of their ability to challenge the hurtful beliefs they have about themselves. They may need to hear that the abuse was not their fault (and why), and also that they can trust their memories about what happened. This lets clients begin trusting in themselves and their decision-making ability.

It is important for them to know that it doesn't matter if the abuse was overt or covert, fondling or intercourse, one time or many times—it still was not their fault. But it isn't just the abuse that is hurtful; as bad as or worse than the abuse is the betrayal by a trusted person, the shame of being used, and feeling powerless and yet responsible. Survivors may feel even more shame if they responded pleasurably to sexual touches. They need to hear it was a *normal* response—that's what bodies do, respond to stimuli.

Survivors Can Reclaim Feeling Like Sexual People

They can be noticed and be attractive without fearing sexual violation. This is an area that requires much more work after primary treatment. If they are in sexual relationships they need to be able to remind themselves that present partners are not the abusers from their pasts. This will help them see if their present relationship feels like an abusive repeat, as it many times may be, or if it is loving and respectful. It will also be helpful in the future if they are able to tell their partners about their abuse so that their partners can give them support for their changes. Suggest that they wait until it feels safe, and if it seems as though it will never feel safe, they probably need to question whether they are in a positive relationship. Some survivors have very supportive partners, others do not. I recommend that if they feel the information will be used against them, they do not share it with their partners. Instead, they can use their recovering friends and professionals as their main outlets. Many need to get permission from other survivors not to be sexual for a while and to feel the right to stop and say no if being sexual is scaring them or reminding them of the abuse.

Abuse Is a Cultural and Social Issue

It's a good idea to remind all women clients that the abuse of children and women is prevalent and is a cultural and social issue. Moreover, it needs to be addressed by all of us. The sexualization and victimization of females pervades our culture at all levels, from churches, to newspapers, to broadcast media, to books that children read, to television advertising for almost any product. Have women look at the cultural dynamics that set them up to be valued only as sexual beings. Some survivors believe so fully that their worth and power are only as sexual beings that they become sexually active in order to have power and have people, men in particular, approve of them and give them affection. It is important that male survivors be reminded that they too have feelings. In our macho-oriented culture, they may not have been allowed to have feelings other than being angry and sexual. Consequently, they look to get many of their emotional needs met on a sexual level. Men must learn other ways to get and give support and affection from friends and lovers.

Survivors Develop Coping Skills

Survivors need to recognize and know that they have creative coping skills. They have been resourceful in surviving by repressing their abuse and dissociating—from the time the abuse first happened. Mistrust, distance from others, the use of alcohol and other drugs, were all seen as ways to get by. They need to hear that they *are survivors* and that they developed creative coping skills for survival. Some of those past coping behaviors—such as chemical abuse—may now be hindering them.

A New Plan

The old family blueprints can be challenged and rewritten. Survivors do not have to live their lives as their parents did—nor raise their children as they were raised. They are not destined to be bad parents. If they feel guilty about things they have done to their families, they can make amends, change, and, we hope, move on.

Feelings Must Be Processed

Last, survivors need to know they have a right to their feelings. Many people they meet in AA or other recovering support groups may push them to give up their anger and resentments, not to dwell in the past. It is true that it is important for them to move on from anger and resentments over past abuse, but ONLY when they are ready. It is a process, and they get to go through it however they need to, at whatever pace feels right.

The Last Stage of Treatment—Aftercare Planning

You can help set the stage for survivors to have a strong sobriety by guiding them to therapy for sexual abuse after they complete chemical dependency treatment. Encourage them to set some simple, immediate goals that will give them more serenity and peace in their sobriety.

Help them look at what might prevent them from taking care of themselves and staying sober. For some, leaving the relative safety of treatment will mean going home to an abusive relationship. Some may still have flashbacks or other memories of their abuse. An aftercare support group is the number one priority for these survivors. Having support and friends is doubly important for those who are in abusive relationships and are alienated from their families.

There are many books on sexual abuse, and some are quite helpful, but it is most important to refer your client to a therapist who understands both chemical dependency and childhood sexual abuse. Such a person can help survivors pace out their recovery. If there are no continuing services at your treatment center or other available mental health services, clients can choose to use self-help groups specifically for abuse survivors. On page 64 is a listing that can guide survivors to groups.

There are treatment programs for women who have been abused. It's important that survivors join a program specifically dedicated to dealing with sexual abuse, and that they don't try to piggyback their recovery from sexual abuse on chemical dependency recovery programs. The abuse issue and chemical dependency are two separate and distinct problems, even though their dynamics can be interrelated.

There are, of course, numerous self-help groups for recovering alcoholics. Survivors are almost sure to meet others who were abused. But be aware that some groups and individuals push people to forgive and forget too quickly, for fear their continuing anger will lead to using alcohol and other drugs again.

Without intervention and recovery, many negative feelings and emotions can be carried around by survivors for a lifetime, particularly the feeling that the world is a scary, uncaring place—with little hope of its getting better. These feelings can keep clients from feeling they have much of a future, even if they are in chemical dependency recovery. The chemical dependency professional is oftentimes the first link in the recovery process for survivors. The most motivated recovering women who come for childhood sexual abuse therapy are those who were encouraged and listened to by their primary chemical dependency treatment counselor. What you do and how you work with women who suffer from both chemical dependency and childhood sexual abuse is extremely important in their recovery. We hope the information in this book will help you better serve those clients dealing with the dual problems of childhood sexual abuse and chemical dependency.

APPENDIX A

Resources

INCEST SURVIVORS
ANONYMOUS
P.O. Box 5613
Long Beach, CA 90805-0613

Advocacy work and referrals:

NATIONAL ORGANIZATION
FOR VICTIM ASSISTANCE
(NOVA)
Suite 200
717 D Street N.W.
Washington, DC 20004

Counseling for survivors and
families:

AMACU (Adults Molested as
Children)
c/o Parents United
P.O. Box 952
San Jose, CA 95108
1-408-280-5055

A forum for survivors to share
their thoughts and arts with
others:

INCEST SURVIVOR INFOR-
MATION EXCHANGE
P.O. Box 3399
New Haven, CT 06515

Survivors can find additional help through local or regional
women's centers, sexual assault centers, and county social
services.

Endnotes

1. Susan Forward and Craig Buck, *Betrayal of Innocence* (New York: Penguin), 1978.
2. Patrick W. Edwards, Ph.D. and Maryann Donaldson, MSW, *Child Abuse and Neglect*, vol. 13 (1989), 101-10.
3. Peter Dimock and Euan Bear, *Adults Molested as Children: A Survivor's Manual for Women and Men* (Shafer Society Press), 1988.
4. Edwards, *Child Abuse and Neglect*.
5. *Diagnostic and Statistical Manual of Mental Disorders*, 3rd ed. (Washington, D.C.: American Psychiatric Association), 1987.
6. Kristin A. Kunzman, *The Healing Way: Adult Recovery from Childhood Sexual Abuse* (Center City, Minn.: Hazelden Educational Materials), 1990.

Suggested Reading

Barbach, Lonnie. *For Yourself: The Fulfillment of Female Sexuality.* Garden City, N.Y.: Anchor Books, 1976.

Bass, Ellen, and Laura Davis. *The Courage to Heal.* New York: Harper & Row, 1988.

Butler, Sandra. *Conspiracy of Silence: The Trauma of Incest.* San Francisco: Volcano Press, 1985.

Caruso, Beverly. *The Impact of Incest.* Center City, Minn.: Hazelden Educational Materials, 1987.

Dimock, Peter, and Euan Bear. *Adults Molested as Children: A Survivor's Manual for Women and Men.* Shafer Society Press, 1988.

Finkelhor, David. *Sexually Victimized Children.* New York: Free Press, 1979.

Forward, Susan, and Craig Buck. *Betrayal of Innocence.* New York: Penguin, 1978.

Herman, Judith. *Father-Daughter Incest.* Cambridge, Mass.: Harvard University Press, 1982.

Kunzman, Kristin. *Healing from Childhood Sexual Abuse.* Center City, Minn.: Hazelden Educational Materials, 1990.

Kunzman, Kristin. *The Healing Way: Adult Recovery from Childhood Sexual Abuse.* Center City, Minn.: Hazelden Educational Materials, 1990.

Maltz, Wendy, and Beverly Holman. *Incest and Sexuality.* Lexington, Mass.: Lexington Books, 1987.

Miller, Alice. *For Your Own Good: Hidden Cruelty in Child Rearing and the Roots of Violence.* New York: Farrar, Straus & Giroux, 1980.

Rush, Florence. *The Best Kept Secret: Sexual Abuse of Children.* Englewood Cliffs, N.J.: Prentice Hall, 1980.

Russell, Diana. *The Secret Trauma: Incest in the Lives of Girls and Women.* New York: Basic Books, 1986.

Other titles that will interest you. . .

Behind the Veil of Silence
Family Violence and Alcohol Abuse
by Beverly Rainbolt and Michael Greene
This pamphlet provides a comprehensive overview of the connection between alcohol abuse and family violence. The authors explain how the two interact, and stress that both alcohol abuse and violence are primary disorders, needing to be treated separately. An excellent resource for those working with abused women. 44 pp.
Order No. 5278

The Impact of Incest
by Beverly Caruso
Incest is among the most common forms of sexual abuse. Now, Beverly Caruso provides incest survivors with general information about incest, including what it is, why it happens, and who it happens to. She also offers guidelines to help survivors recover, and suggests ways to find help. 48 pp.
Order No. 5457

The Healing Way
Adult Recovery from Childhood Sexual Abuse
by Kristin A. Kunzman
For the therapist and the abuse survivor, this book is a fundamental resource of self-care information, recovery issues, and encouragement for working at healing. The author discusses, among other topics, reclaiming a healthy sexuality, stopping abusive child-rearing cycles, and grieving the past.
Order No. 5083

**For price and order information, or a free catalog,
please call our Telephone Representatives.**

HAZELDEN EDUCATIONAL MATERIALS

1-800-328-9000   **1-612-257-4010**   **1-612-257-2195**

(Toll Free. U.S., Canada,   (Outside the U.S.)   (FAX)
and the Virgin Islands)   and Canada)

Pleasant Valley Road • P.O. Box 176 • Center City, MN 55012-0176

**HAZELDEN EDUCATIONAL SERVICES INTERNATIONAL
Cork, Ireland • Int'l Code + 353-21-961-269**